A DOZEN PLUS REASONS WHY YOU SHOULD LEARN TO DO YOUR OWN TAXES

By

Milton G. Boothe, EA

I0489314

Table of Contents

1. The Benefits of Doing Your Own Taxes

Doing your own taxes is not as difficult a task as your tax professional might want you to perceive it to be. Actually, tax preparation software has come a long way in the past few years, making it so easy for you to prepare your own taxes, that it's virtually impossible not to be able to understand the process, even with absolutely no knowledge of tax laws. This holds particularly true with tax preparation software such as **Turbo Tax, Tax Act, Tax Slayer,** and **H & R Block at Home,** just to name of few. Tax software has gotten even better, and is relatively inexpensive, so it is virtually just as easy and effective to use tax software as it is to go to a professional tax preparer.

Actually, there are significant benefits to be derived from doing your own taxes.

- Doing your own taxes means that you do not have to disclose your sensitive personal information to another person, and this is significant, because you will eliminate the risk of having your information falling into the wrong hands. Do you know how safe is your personal information is after you leave them with your tax preparer? The IRS is grappling with a five-fold increase in taxpayer identity theft between 2008 and 2011, and is advising that if you use tax accountants, you should query them on what measures they take to protect your information.
- Doing your own taxes will actually save you a bundle. Hiring an accountant these days can be costly; tax preparation fees can range from $300 and upwards for an average tax return with a Schedule A.
- Doing your own taxes places you in full control of your tax return. Because you can work on your taxes at your own pace, you can take as much time as you want, and do whatever research is necessary to ensure optimum results, which of course can literally translate into thousands of dollars in your pocket each year.
- Doing your own taxes will motivate you to take a closer look at your own finances, and as you immerse yourself in the process, you will gradually become more knowledgeable about tax matters and money management issues.

To maximize the benefits of doing your own taxes, however, it is obvious that you will need to have a certain amount of basic tax knowledge. Although the software will try to guide you through the process in some way or another, to ensure that you will claim all your tax credits and deductions, it would be to your advantage if you could place yourself in a position that will allow you to be somewhat proactive, as far as being able to identify all your eligible tax credits and deductions, even before you begin your return.

Let's face it; tax credits and deductions can be worth a lot these days! For example, the Earned Income Credit can be worth up to almost $6,000 if you have three or more kids, and your income falls within a certain range. If you were to miss out on this credit, and on any of the many others that you might be eligible for, that would be an absolute tragedy! It would be like giving your money away to the government just like that!

There are certain rules laid down by the IRS, which determine the taxpayer's eligibility to claim all relevant tax credits and deductions that exist. Without knowledge of these rules, however, you might be at risk of losing out on some of these tax credits and deductions that you could be eligible for.

To help you with the entire process of preparing your tax returns, and to give you a thorough understanding of the rules which determine your eligibility for the various tax credits and deductions, there is an entire series of tax publications, which are currently available for the 2013 tax season, and which have been compiled in simple layman terms.

"Doing Your Own Taxes is as Easy as 1, 2, 3." will be available from mid-January 2014 in the following bookstores:

1) Amazon.com, in both Kindle and paperback formats.
2) Barnes & Noble
3) Apple iBookstore
4) Sony Reader Store
5) Kobo
6) Copia
7) Gardners
8) Baker & Taylor
9) eBookPie
10) eSentral
11) Scribd
12) PagePusher

If you are specifically interested in only certain areas of the tax return, you might find these shorter publications to be particularly useful. These following titles are also available on **Amazon.com** in both **Kindle** and **paperback** formats:

"A Comprehensive Guide to Claiming All Your Tax Credits and Deductions for Tax Year 2013."

> *"A Comprehensive Guide to Reporting All Your Income for Tax Year 2013."*
>
> *"Understanding Your Taxes: Your Business and Rental Income, and Your Deduction for Depreciation."*
>
> *"Understanding Your Taxes: Your Non-business Income and Your Adjustments to Income."*
>
> *"Understanding Your Taxes: Social Security, Retirement Instruments, and Capital Gains."*
>
> *"Understanding Your Taxes: Tax Credits, Itemized Deductions, and the Standard Deduction."*
>
> *"Understanding Your Taxes: The 1040 Tax Return, Your Filing Status, and Your Personal and Dependency Exemptions."*
>
> *"Understanding Your Taxes: Other Miscellaneous Tax Matters."*

These publications aim to educate you, the taxpayer, on how you can "optimize" your tax return. Optimizing your tax return, essentially means claiming all the deductions and credits that you are legally entitled to, thus maximizing your tax refund, or minimizing your tax liability, if one exists.

These publications will effectively equip you with a good basic knowledge of the tax code, so that you will be in the position to protect your cash flows, as far as your dealings with the IRS is concerned.

No longer do you have to be daunted by the complexity of the tax code. Unlike most other tax publications, these publications have been compiled specifically with the taxpayer in mind, and although very comprehensive, they are also concise, and very easy to understand. These publications are very "reader friendly"—having been compiled in layman's terms, using simple language, and avoiding tax jargon as much as possible, as they break down the relevant areas of the tax code into understandable segments. The reader, therefore, does not need to have any prior tax knowledge to easily follow what's contained therein.

These publications explain **every** line on the Form 1040 tax return, and in doing so, makes it absolutely clear that preparing your own taxes is not as daunting a task as many of you might perceive it to be. So, for those of you who wish to take on the challenge and prepare your tax returns yourself, you will definitely find these publications to be a very powerful resource tool. Following the guidelines in these publications will enable you to prepare almost any Form 1040 tax return. Furthermore, you need to take into account even the basic savings you can enjoy by just doing it yourself. (The average cost of preparing a typical 1040 tax return can be upwards of $400.)

If you plan to prepare your tax returns yourself, it is strongly recommended, however, that you purchase off-the-shelf tax software, which is now relatively cheap. There are usually a number of schedules and worksheets that need to be completed with most tax returns, some of which can be relatively complex (which you will see as you go through these publications). Off-the-shelf tax software will accurately and effectively complete these schedules/worksheets for you, some of which you probably wouldn't be able to do manually, unless you were a trained tax professional. Also, off-the-shelf tax software affords you the ability to electronically file your returns from the comfort of your homes. Off-the-shelf tax software will also effectively prepare your state tax returns for you, if you live in a state that imposes income tax.

2. Why You Should Learn to Do Your Own Taxes

When we talk about saving money by learning to do our own taxes, we are not just talking about the $300 or $400 that could probably be saved by not having to pay our tax preparers. What we are actually talking about is the thousands of dollars which we can potentially lose each year if our tax preparers do not claim all the critical tax credits and deductions that we are legally entitled to; and this is just like giving away our money to the government.

It is a fact that every year, millions of taxpayers in the USA collectively lose millions of dollars to the government. This unfortunate scenario basically exists because of ignorance on their part, which of course in understandable, but more preposterously, because of ignorance or negligence on the part of the professionals they have paid to prepare their tax returns.

This incidence of erroneously prepared income tax returns is now of such a magnitude that the IRS has had to step in and take action. Consequently, as of 2013, anyone who prepares tax returns for a fee, unless he or she is a CPA, attorney, or enrolled agent, will have to be certified by the IRS. Such a person will have to pass an IRS competency examination and a background check, before this certification can be obtained. This IRS ruling, however, is currently being challenged in the courts, and if the opponents prevail, this will surely be to the detriment of the taxpayer who relies on his or her paid preparer.

Millions of taxpayers rely on the expertise of these well-known and popular national tax preparation companies and franchises that operate across the USA. People tend to place their confidence in these companies and franchises, when the IRS, based upon its actions, implicitly appears to be of the perception that there is a serious lack of expertise in the tax preparation industry today.

The fact is; many employees of these national tax companies and franchises are not adequately trained for the job you pay them to do. The reality is that many of these employees are usually only given a "crash course" in tax preparation, and are then put behind a computer, where they present themselves to the public as tax professionals, when in the true sense of the word they probably are not. Tax laws, in reality, are numerous and are very complex, and it's virtually impossible for an average human being who has had no prior knowledge of tax law, to grasp the entire significance of the U.S. tax code from a mere six week course.

It is also a fact that these tax companies/franchises do not offer attractive compensation to prospective employees, and this makes it extremely difficult for them to attract competent professionals.

Because they have not been adequately trained, these tax preparers now rely solely on the tax software made available to them by their employers, and not on professional knowledge; hence, it boils down to the old proverbial scenario of "garbage in – garbage out." This probably is the angle from which the IRS is currently viewing the situation.

From your perspective as a taxpayer, the bottom line is that an improperly prepared tax return is going to end up costing you in one way or the other. If your tax preparer does not claim all the credits and deductions that you are legally entitled to, you will end up receiving a lower tax refund or incurring a higher tax liability, and that basically means giving away your money to the government. One the other hand, if your tax preparer makes claims on your tax return that legally should not have been made, it's going to cost you also, in the way of unnecessary penalties and interest. Yet, at the end of the day, you can be absolutely sure that your tax preparer is going to present you with a bill for his or her services.

The fact of the matter is that you can literally save hundreds of dollars each year, and probably even thousands, just by being in the position to be able to ensure that your tax returns have been properly prepared.

Failure to claim all your tax credits and deductions can literally result in you losing thousands of dollars each year. For example, let us take a look at the Earned Income Credit. This is a tax credit, which can be valued at over $6,000 for lower income earners with three or more qualifying children. But even if you even do not have any qualifying children, you are still eligible for some of this credit if your income sits within the specified range. It is indeed very unsettling to realize that some seasoned tax preparers actually miss out on even this basic tax credit.

In addition to the Earned Income tax credit, there is a whole series of tax credits and deductions that many taxpayers can significantly benefit from, but which tax preparers oftentimes overlook. Some of these include the following:
- Credit for child and dependent care expenses
- The additional child tax credit
- Credit for excess Social Security Tax
- Foreign tax credit
- Adoption credit
- Non-business energy property credit
- Credit for the elderly and disabled
- Alternative motor vehicle credits (for hybrid vehicles)

- General business credits
- Education credits (American Opportunity and Lifetime Learning credits)
- Student loan interest deduction
- Tuition and fees deduction
- Medical and dental expense deduction
- Mortgage interest deduction
- Property tax deduction
- Cash contributions to charity
- Non-cash contributions to charity (such as donating your car)
- Casualty and theft losses deduction
- Deductions for losses on deposits held in insolvent financial institutions
- Deductions for losses from Ponzi-type investment schemes
- Employee Travel expenses deduction
- Employee meal and entertainment expenses
- Employee business gift expenses deduction
- Employee local transportation deduction
- Car expenses deduction
- Business use of your home deduction
- Job-related education expenses deduction
- Moving expenses deduction
- IRA contribution deduction
- One-half of self-employment tax deduction
- Self-employed health insurance deduction
- Self-employed qualified retirement plans deduction
- Health savings account deduction
- Educator expenses deduction
- Penalty on early withdrawal of savings deduction
- Alimony paid deduction
- Domestic production activities deduction
- Business expenses of reservists, performing artists, and fee-based government officials

Empowering yourself with basic tax knowledge will place you in the position to know about **ALL** the credits and deductions that you are legally entitled to, based on your particular circumstances. Even if you decide not to do your own taxes, you will be in the position to determine whether your tax preparer has done a good job, by including on your tax return, all the tax credits and deductions that you are eligible for.

3. The 1040 Tax Return Explained: It's Not as Difficult as it Seems

Preparing your own taxes is not as daunting a task as many of you might perceive it to be. As a matter of fact, doing your own taxes can be as easy as 1, 2, 3. Also, if you decide to do your own taxes, you could probably end up saving thousands of dollars in the process.

Most individuals earning income in the U.S. must file a tax return. This is the law. Most individuals file a tax return using Form 1040, *U.S. Individual Income Tax Return.* At first glance, the Form 1040 will typically be perceived to be a very complex government form, which can only be completed by trained tax professionals. This is a great misconception, although your tax professional might want you to think this way. That is true only to a small extent, because in actual fact, if you were to take some time to peruse this form in detail, you would probably discover that more than 90% of what's on the form will be totally irrelevant to you. Typically, after identifying the lines that are relevant to you, you will be pleasantly surprised to discover just how easy it is to do your own taxes.

Some individuals, depending on their circumstances, may be able to file Form 1040A, a modified version of Form 1040, or Form 1040EZ, *Income Tax Return for Single and Joint Filers with No Dependents,* instead of Form 1040. Both these forms are shorter versions of Form 1040, and can be used in the following situations:

- You can use Form 1040A if your taxable income is below $100,000 and you take the standard deduction instead of itemizing deductions.
- You can use Form 1040EZ if: (a) you have no dependents, (b) your taxable income is below $100,000, and (c) you take the standard deduction instead of itemizing deductions.

The 1040 Tax Return

In this chapter, we will concentrate on Form 1040, which is the more commonly used one. This form is comprised of a number of sections, and we shall proceed to review each section in detail, to provide an overview of the structure of the U.S. individual tax return.

The Information Section

Tax year
For most individuals this will be the calendar year (January 1 to December 31, 2013). If your tax year ends other than on December 31, 2013, you must report it here.

Name, address, and Social Security number
You enter your name, address, and Social Security number in this section. If you are married you must enter the Social Security number of your spouse also, even if you are not filing a joint return. If you receive a preprinted label provided by the IRS, you may use that label here.

Filing Status and Exemptions

Filing Status
You must identify your filing status from the five options contained in this section, by checking the appropriate box. You can check only one box. Your filing status determines a number of things, such as:

- Whether you must file a return.
- Your standard deduction.
- Your tax rate.
- Your eligibility for certain deductions and credits.

13

Exemptions

Each taxpayer is entitled to a certain number of tax exemptions, depending on their particular circumstances. You claim all your exemptions in this section of the form. Your exemptions reduce the amount of your income that is taxed. In figuring the total number of exemptions that you are entitled to, you should list yourself (unless someone else is claiming you as a dependent on their return), your spouse (if any), and any dependents you are claiming. Each dependent must have a valid Social Security number or an individual taxpayer identification number (ITIN) if you are to claim this person as a dependent. You must check the appropriate boxes, and report your total exemptions on line 6d.

The Income Section

Income						
Attach Form(s) W-2 here. Also attach Forms W-2G and 1099-R if tax was withheld.	7	Wages, salaries, tips, etc. Attach Form(s) W-2			7	
	8a	**Taxable** interest. Attach Schedule B if required			8a	
	b	**Tax-exempt** interest. **Do not** include on line 8a	**8b**			
	9a	Ordinary dividends. Attach Schedule B if required			9a	
	b	Qualified dividends	**9b**			
	10	Taxable refunds, credits, or offsets of state and local income taxes			10	
If you did not get a W-2, see instructions.	11	Alimony received			11	
	12	Business income or (loss). Attach Schedule C or C-EZ			12	
	13	Capital gain or (loss). Attach Schedule D if required. If not required, check here ▶ ☐			13	
	14	Other gains or (losses). Attach Form 4797			14	
	15a	IRA distributions	**15a**	b Taxable amount	15b	
	16a	Pensions and annuities	**16a**	b Taxable amount	16b	
	17	Rental real estate, royalties, partnerships, S corporations, trusts, etc. Attach Schedule E			17	
	18	Farm income or (loss). Attach Schedule F			18	
	19	Unemployment compensation			19	
	20a	Social security benefits	**20a**	b Taxable amount	20b	
	21	Other income. List type and amount			21	
	22	Combine the amounts in the far right column for lines 7 through 21. This is your **total income** ▶			22	

Most income that you receive is taxable. You report your income from all sources on lines 7 through 21, in this section of the form. Some income must be figured first on other forms and schedules (which we shall see later) before taken to the income section. Also, some income is nontaxable, and is usually not reported (for example, child support). You report your total taxable income on line 22.

Adjusted Gross Income

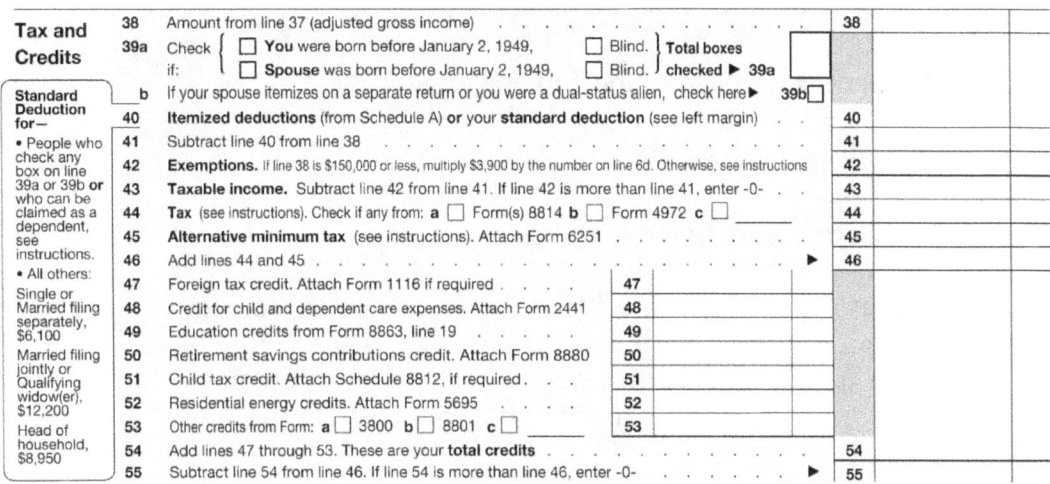

Adjusted Gross Income	23	Educator expenses	23
	24	Certain business expenses of reservists, performing artists, and fee-basis government officials. Attach Form 2106 or 2106-EZ	24
	25	Health savings account deduction. Attach Form 8889	25
	26	Moving expenses. Attach Form 3903	26
	27	Deductible part of self-employment tax. Attach Schedule SE	27
	28	Self-employed SEP, SIMPLE, and qualified plans	28
	29	Self-employed health insurance deduction	29
	30	Penalty on early withdrawal of savings	30
	31a	Alimony paid b Recipient's SSN ▶	31a
	32	IRA deduction	32
	33	Student loan interest deduction	33
	34	Tuition and fees. Attach Form 8917	34
	35	Domestic production activities deduction. Attach Form 8903	35
	36	Add lines 23 through 35	36
	37	Subtract line 36 from line 22. This is your **adjusted gross income** ▶	37

You list all your eligible adjustments to your gross income on lines 23 through 35 of this section. Adjustments are subtracted from the total income reported on line 22, thus reducing your taxable income, and ultimately your tax liability. Examples of adjustments to gross income include; penalty on early withdrawal of savings, IRA deduction, student loan interest deduction, tuition and fees deduction, moving expenses, alimony paid, etc.

Your **Adjusted Gross Income (AGI)** is figured on line 37, by subtracting your total adjustments on line 36 from your total income on line 22.

Tax and Credits

Tax and Credits	38	Amount from line 37 (adjusted gross income)	38
	39a	Check if: ☐ You were born before January 2, 1949, ☐ Blind. ☐ Spouse was born before January 2, 1949, ☐ Blind. Total boxes checked ▶ 39a	
Standard Deduction for—	b	If your spouse itemizes on a separate return or you were a dual-status alien, check here ▶ 39b ☐	
• People who check any box on line 39a or 39b or who can be claimed as a dependent, see instructions.	40	**Itemized deductions** (from Schedule A) **or** your **standard deduction** (see left margin)	40
	41	Subtract line 40 from line 38	41
	42	**Exemptions.** If line 38 is $150,000 or less, multiply $3,900 by the number on line 6d. Otherwise, see instructions	42
	43	**Taxable income.** Subtract line 42 from line 41. If line 42 is more than line 41, enter -0-	43
	44	**Tax** (see instructions). Check if any from: **a** ☐ Form(s) 8814 **b** ☐ Form 4972 **c** ☐	44
• All others: Single or Married filing separately, $6,100	45	**Alternative minimum tax** (see instructions). Attach Form 6251	45
	46	Add lines 44 and 45 ▶	46
Married filing jointly or Qualifying widow(er), $12,200	47	Foreign tax credit. Attach Form 1116 if required	47	
	48	Credit for child and dependent care expenses. Attach Form 2441	48	
	49	Education credits from Form 8863, line 19	49	
	50	Retirement savings contributions credit. Attach Form 8880	50	
Head of household, $8,950	51	Child tax credit. Attach Schedule 8812, if required	51	
	52	Residential energy credits. Attach Form 5695	52	
	53	Other credits from Form: **a** ☐ 3800 **b** ☐ 8801 **c** ☐	53	
	54	Add lines 47 through 53. These are your **total credits**	54
	55	Subtract line 54 from line 46. If line 54 is more than line 46, enter -0- ▶	55

If you are over 65, and/or blind, you are entitled to a higher *standard deduction*. Therefore, on line 39a, you should check the appropriate boxes if you or your spouse were born before January 2, 1949. If either you or your spouse is blind, you should also check the appropriate boxes. Checking any of these boxes will entitle you to a higher standard deduction.

On line 40, you enter either your *standard deduction* or your *itemized deductions,* but not both. The amount of your *standard deduction* is determined by your filing status, your age, and whether you are legally blind. Your *itemized deductions* consist of certain qualifying expenditure you incur, that the IRS will allow you to deduct in place of your *standard deduction*, if they are in excess of your *standard deduction*. If you are married and you are filing a separate return from your spouse, you must check line 39b if your spouse itemizes deductions.

You figure your total exemption amount by multiplying the total number of exemptions you claim on line 6d by $3,900. You are entitled to one exemption amount for each dependent, plus the exemption amounts for yourself, and for your spouse, if you are filing a joint return.

To figure your taxable income, you subtract your *standard deduction* (or *itemized deductions*) plus your exemptions, from your AGI. You report your taxable income on line 43. At this stage of the return, you figure your tax by using the tax tables, and you report the amount of tax figured on line 44.

Depending on your particular circumstances, you might be eligible for some tax credits. Some of the tax credits for which you might be eligible for are reported on lines 47 through 53. These credits are termed nonrefundable credits, and are deducted from your tax figured on line 44, thus ultimately increasing your tax refund, or reducing your tax liability, if one exists. Nonrefundable tax credits include the following:
- Foreign tax credit.
- Credit for child and dependent care expenses.
- Some education credits.
- Retirement savings contribution credit.
- Child tax credit.
- Residential energy credit.

You total these credits on line 54, subtract them from your tax on line 46, and enter the result on line 55.

It is very important to understand that the credits in this section are all *non-refundable* credits, meaning that if they exceed the amount of the tax, you <u>cannot</u> receive a refund for the unused part of these credits, if any. These credits can only reduce your tax to zero, and that's where they stop.

Other Taxes

Other	56	Self-employment tax. Attach Schedule SE	56	
Taxes	57	Unreported social security and Medicare tax from Form: **a** ☐ 4137 **b** ☐ 8919 . .	57	
	58	Additional tax on IRAs, other qualified retirement plans, etc. Attach Form 5329 if required . .	58	
	59a	Household employment taxes from Schedule H	59a	
	b	First-time homebuyer credit repayment. Attach Form 5405 if required	59b	
	60	Taxes from: **a** ☐ Form 8959 **b** ☐ Form 8960 **c** ☐ Instructions; enter code(s) _____	60	
	61	Add lines 55 through 60. This is your **total tax** . . . . ▶	61	

There are some other taxes that you may be liable for, depending on your circumstances, and these taxes include the following:
- Self-employed tax.
- Unreported Social Security and Medicare tax.
- Additional tax on IRAs.
- Household employment taxes.
- First-time homebuyer credit repayment.

You report these other taxes on lines 56 through 60, and they must be added to the amount on line 55, to figure your total tax, which you report on line 61.

Payments

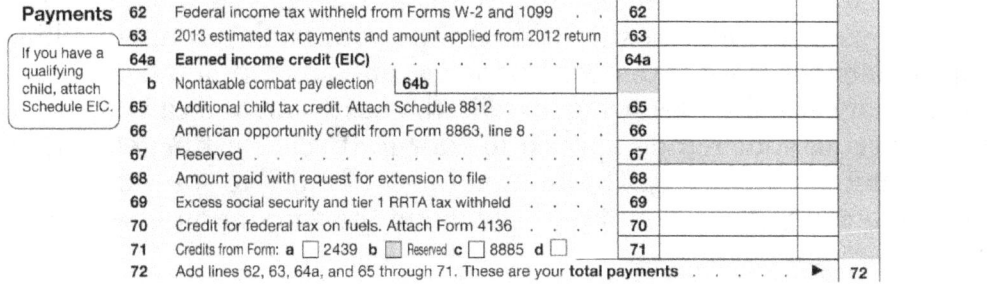

Payments	62	Federal income tax withheld from Forms W-2 and 1099 . .	62	
	63	2013 estimated tax payments and amount applied from 2012 return	63	
If you have a qualifying child, attach Schedule EIC.	64a	**Earned income credit (EIC)**	64a	
	b	Nontaxable combat pay election | 64b |		
	65	Additional child tax credit. Attach Schedule 8812	65	
	66	American opportunity credit from Form 8863, line 8	66	
	67	Reserved	67	
	68	Amount paid with request for extension to file	68	
	69	Excess social security and tier 1 RRTA tax withheld	69	
	70	Credit for federal tax on fuels. Attach Form 4136	70	
	71	Credits from Form: **a** ☐ 2439 **b** ☐ Reserved **c** ☐ 8885 **d** ☐ ___	71	
	72	Add lines 62, 63, 64a, and 65 through 71. These are your **total payments** . . . . ▶	72	

Your payments include all federal tax payments you have already made during the year, and include the following:
- Taxes withheld from your salary by your employer. This is reported to you on Form W-2.
- Any tax withheld from amounts paid to you by any other payer.
- Any estimated tax payments that you made directly to the IRS during the tax year.

Certain other credits that you might be eligible for are also included in the payments section of the form. These credits are termed *refundable credits,* and are also classified as payments. *Refundable credits* include the following:
- Earned income credit.
- Additional child tax credit.
- American opportunity credit.

- Credit for federal tax on fuels.
- Excess Social Security and tier 1 RRTA tax withheld.

Refundable credits are added together with your payments, and this total is entered on line 72.

In contrast to *nonrefundable* credits, *refundable* credits <u>will</u> result in a tax refund if they exceed your total tax (see below).

Refund/Amount You Owe

Refund	73	If line 72 is more than line 61, subtract line 61 from line 72. This is the amount you **overpaid**		73	
	74a	Amount of line 73 you want **refunded to you.** If Form 8888 is attached, check here ► ☐		74a	
Direct deposit? ► b		Routing number ►c Type: ☐ Checking ☐ Savings			
See instructions. ► d		Account number			
	75	Amount of line 73 you want **applied to your 2014 estimated tax** ► 75			
Amount	76	**Amount you owe.** Subtract line 72 from line 61. For details on how to pay, see instructions ►		76	
You Owe	77	Estimated tax penalty (see instructions) 77			

Refund
If the total of your payments and *refundable* credits (line 72) exceed your total tax (line 61), this represents an overpayment of taxes on your part, and is reported on line 73. If you have an amount on line 73, this means you are entitled to a tax refund of this amount from the IRS. If you wish, you can choose to have your refund deposited directly into your bank account by filling in the appropriate boxes with your bank's routing and account number.
If you figure that you might be owing taxes in the next year, you can choose to have all or a part of your refund applied to your next year's estimated tax, by entering that amount on line 75. The amount to be refunded to you will now be the difference between the amount on line 73 and the amount on line 75, and you enter that amount on line 74a.

Amount you owe
If the total tax (line 61) exceeds your total payments and *refundable* credits (line 72), this means that there was an underpayment of taxes on your part. This underpayment is reported on line 76, and this means that you owe the IRS this amount. Generally, you must send a payment for the amount you owe when you file your taxes, and you may also be charged a penalty.

The Signatures Section

Third Party Designee	Do you want to allow another person to discuss this return with the IRS (see instructions)? ☐ **Yes.** Complete below.		☐ **No**
	Designee's name ▶	Phone no. ▶	Personal identification number (PIN) ▶ ☐☐☐☐☐

Sign Here	Under penalties of perjury, I declare that I have examined this return and accompanying schedules and statements, and to the best of my knowledge and belief, they are true, correct, and complete. Declaration of preparer (other than taxpayer) is based on all information of which preparer has any knowledge.				
Joint return? See instructions. Keep a copy for your records.	Your signature	Date	Your occupation		Daytime phone number
	Spouse's signature. If a joint return, **both** must sign.	Date	Spouse's occupation		If the IRS sent you an Identity Protection PIN, enter it here (see inst.) ☐☐☐☐☐☐

Paid Preparer Use Only	Print/Type preparer's name	Preparer's signature		Date	Check ☐ if self-employed	PTIN
	Firm's name ▶			Firm's EIN ▶		
	Firm's address ▶			Phone no.		

Third party designee
You can allow the IRS to discuss your return with any person you choose, by checking the "Yes" box and completing the requested information.

Taxpayer's signature
You are required to sign your return, and state your occupation. If you are married and are filing a joint return, your spouse must also sign the return in the designated area.

Paid preparer's signature
Your paid preparer will sign in the section designated to him or her.

3. Some Pretty Useful Tips to Help You in Filing Your Taxes This Year

This chapter addresses some of the very basic issues that one would encounter on a typical tax return. It looks at some of the basic exemptions, deductions, and credits that one would expect to claim on a basic return, and also looks at the whole issue of choosing the correct filing status, which is really the first step you take in ensuring that you will end up with a properly prepared tax return.

If your tax return goes into more in-depth and complex issues, then it would be absolutely advisable to procure one of the relevant publications listed in chapter 1.

Filing Status

Choosing the correct filing status is very important, and is really the first step that you take in ensuring that you will end up with an accurately prepared tax return. You need to appreciate this, because your filing status determines a number of very important things, such as; filing requirements, tax deductions, tax credits, tax rate, and ultimately, your correct tax refund or tax liability. In general, filing status depends on whether a taxpayer is considered unmarried or married, and this is determined based on your marital on the last day of the tax year. For federal tax purposes, a marriage means **only** a legal union between a man and a woman as husband and wife. The word *spouse* means a person of the opposite sex who is a husband or a wife.

You must choose from one of five filing statuses, and you must know which one is correct for you. The five filing statuses are: (a) Single, (b) Married Filing Jointly, (c) Married Filing Separately, (d) Head of Household, and (e) Qualifying Widow/Widower. If you discover that more than one filing status applies to you, you may choose the one that gives you the lowest tax rate.

Single

You are required to file *Single* if any of the following conditions apply to you:

- You are unmarried on the last day of the tax year.
- You are divorced or legally separated under a separate maintenance decree on the last day of the tax year.

- You are widowed before the first day of the tax year, and have not remarried during the tax year.

Filing Single generally attracts a higher tax rate, and has a lower standard deduction than some of the other filing statuses. You normally file Single if you do not qualify for any other filing status, but there are some exceptions. If you provide for a child living with you, or if you are a surviving spouse, you may not be required to file Single, and might be able to choose a more favorable filing status, as long as certain other conditions are met. We shall look at these exceptions below.

Married Filing Jointly (MFJ)

Your marital status for the tax year is decided, based upon your marital status on December 31. If a couple is married on December 31 of the tax year; that couple may file a joint return for the year, regardless of when in the year they got married.

Consequently, you can file *Married Filing Jointly* if you and your spouse meet any one of the following tests:

- You are married and living together as husband and wife, on the last day of the tax year.
- You are married on the last day of the tax year and living apart, but are not legally separated under a decree of divorce or separate maintenance.
- Your spouse died during the year, and you did not remarry during the year.
- You are living together in a common law union that is recognized by the state where you live, or in the state where the common law union began.

In order to file a joint return, both spouses are required to:

- Include all their income, exemptions, and deductions on the joint tax return, and
- Use the same accounting period.

The MFJ filing status generally has the lowest rate of tax, and is the more favorable filing status for married couples.

If your spouse died during the tax year, and you remarried during the year, you may file MFJ with your new spouse. You deceased spouse's filing status, however, would have to be *Married Filing Separately*.

Note that tax law does not mandate that a married couple should file a joint tax return; this decision is a matter of choice; they can file separate returns if they wish.

Note also, that to file MFJ, both spouses do not need to have income to file jointly, however, both spouses are responsible for the joint return, and both must sign the return.

Married Filing Separately (MFS)

If you are married and decide not to file a joint return with your spouse, you must use the *Married Filing Separately* filing status.

There is, however, one very important exception to this rule: A married taxpayer can be *considered unmarried* by law, if he or she maintains a household for a child, and the spouse was not a member of the household for the last six months of the taxable year. Such a taxpayer would not be required to file MFS, but could be able to file as *Head of Household* (see below).

Although filing a joint return generally produces lower taxes, the opposite can sometimes be the case, and to maximize the tax advantage in such circumstances, married couples may decide to file separately for a particular year. Married taxpayers, therefore, have the option of filing *Married Filing Separately*, and can consider this option if:

- Each spouse wants to be responsible for his or her taxes only.
- Both spouses agree not to file a joint return.

When you file MFS, you report only your own income, exemptions, credits, and deductions.

You should consider carefully before choosing this option, because filing MFS usually puts you at a disadvantaged position, and usually means paying more taxes than filing MFJ. This is so, because MFS has the highest tax rate. Filing MFS also disqualifies you from most of the tax credits and deductions that are available for the other filing statuses (see below).

If you file MFS, you are required to enter your spouse's full name on line 3 of Form 1040, and also your spouse's Social Security number in the heading section of Form 1040.

You can change a MFS return to a MFJ return within three years, by filing an amended return. You cannot change from MFJ to MFS however.

The Disadvantages of Filing Married Filing Separately

You should consider carefully, before choosing the MFS filing status, because there are some distinct disadvantages in choosing this filing status, and these are as follows:

- You <u>cannot</u> claim the standard deduction (see next chapter) if your spouse itemizes; in this case, you must itemize also. This means then, that you could lose out on a substantial deduction if the expenses that you have to itemize are less than the amount of the standard deduction.
- You cannot claim the credit for child and dependent care expenses in most cases.
- You cannot claim the education credits, the deduction for student loan interest, or the tuition and fees deduction.
- You cannot claim the earned income credit.
- You cannot exclude from income any interest earned from Series EE U.S. Savings Bonds that was used for higher education expenses.
- You cannot claim the credit for adoption expenses in most cases.
- You may have a smaller child tax credit than if you filed jointly.
- Your capital loss deduction is limited to $1,500 (instead of $3,000 for all other filing statuses).

Also, if you lived with your spouse at any time during the year and filed MFS, you:

- Cannot claim the credit for the elderly or the disabled.
- May have to include more Social Security benefits received, in taxable income.
- Cannot roll over amounts from a traditional IRA to a Roth IRA.

Head of Household (HOH)

If you are single, or married but *considered unmarried* (see below) on the last day of the tax year, you can file *Head of Household,* if both conditions below apply to you:

> (a) You paid more than half the costs of keeping up a home for the tax year, and
> (b) A qualified person (see definition below) lived with you for more than half of the tax year.

A taxpayer filing *Head of Household* can have substantial financial benefits over a *Single* status taxpayer. In filing as Head of Household, you will enjoy both a lower tax rate, and a larger Standard Deduction.

In determining the cost of keeping up a home, you may include costs such as mortgage interest, real estate tax, home insurance, repairs, utilities, and food. You cannot include amounts you paid for clothing, education, medical treatment, vacations, life insurance, transportation, or the rental value of your home. In determining the amount you paid in keeping up the home, you must exclude any payments received from public assistance.

Definition of a Qualifying Person

To choose the Head of Household filing status, the general rule is that you must have a *qualifying person* living with you for at least half of the year. A qualifying person includes any of the following:

- An unmarried child, including your own child, grandchild, stepchild, or foster child. The child does not necessarily have to be a dependent on your tax return, but must live with you. (For example, the child could be claimed by the other parent, but you would still be able to claim the Head of Household filing status, as long as the child lived with you.)
- A married child, including your own child, grandchild, stepchild, or foster child. In this case, the child must be a dependent on your tax return.
- A relative who is a dependent on your tax return, such as your parent, grandparent, brother, sister, stepbrother, stepsister, half-brother or half-sister, niece or nephew.

Note that a person, who is your qualifying relative, ONLY because he or she lived with you as a member of your household (no blood or marriage relationship) for the entire year, CANNOT qualify you for the HOH filing status. For example: a live-in boyfriend or girlfriend, or boyfriend's or girlfriend's child does not qualify you for HOH. Neither does a cousin qualify you for HOH.

Parent Not Living With You

There is one exception to the rule that your dependent must live with you to qualify you for the Head of Household filing status. You can file as Head of Household even if your parent does not physically live with you, as long as you paid more than half the cost of keeping up a home that was the parent's main home for the entire year. For example, your parent could be living in a rest home or home for the elderly.

Temporary Absence

You and your qualifying person are still considered to live together even if one or both of you are temporary absent from the home, due to special circumstances such as illness, education, business, vacation, or military service.

Married Considered Unmarried

This is a very important exception to the rule that married people, who decide not to file a joint return together, must file Married Filing Separately. If you are married and separated from your spouse, under tax law you may be *considered unmarried,* if certain conditions are met. This means that you could qualify to file HOH instead of MFS, and therefore will not be subject to the disadvantages of the MFS filing status.

Under tax law, you can be *considered unmarried* on the last day of the tax year if you meet all the following tests:

- You must file a separate return from your spouse.
- You must have paid more than half the costs of keeping up a home for the tax year.
- You must not have lived with your spouse at any time during the last 6 months of the tax year.
- Your home must have been the main home for your child, stepchild, or eligible foster child for more than half of the year.
- You must be able to claim an exemption for the child. You still meet this test if the child was not claimed because you allowed the non-custodial parent to claim the exemption for the child.

Qualifying Widow/Widower with Dependent Child (QW)

Surviving spouses receive the same standard deduction and tax rates as taxpayers who are filing Married Filing Jointly. In the year of your spouse's death, if you do not remarry, you can file a joint return with your deceased spouse. For the following two years, you can use the *Qualifying Widow/Widower with Dependent Child* filing status, if you have a dependent child living with you. After two years, if you have not remarried, you must change your filing status to either Single or Head of Household, depending on your circumstances.

You can consider the Qualifying Widow(er) filing status if you are a widow(er) and:

- You could have filed a joint return with your spouse for the year your spouse died.
- Your spouse died in either of the two tax years preceding this current year.
- You have a child or stepchild who qualifies as a dependent. (Note that this does not include a foster child.)
- You paid over half the costs of keeping up a home for the entire year.

- The child lived in your home all year, except for periods of temporary absence.

Note however, that the surviving spouse <u>cannot</u> continue to claim an exemption for the deceased spouse in the two years that he or she is allowed to use the QW filing status; he or she can <u>only</u> claim the filing status, and thus take the same standard deduction as a married couple filing jointly.

Your Personal and Dependent Exemptions

Exemptions directly reduce your taxable income. You are entitled to one personal exemption for yourself, one for your spouse (if filing a joint return), and one exemption for each dependent that you claim on your tax return. Knowing the criteria and requirements for claiming these exemptions will facilitate the preparation of your individual income tax return, and will ensure that you do not miss out on important tax benefits.

Exemptions are fixed amounts, calculated on a per person basis, and they reduce the amount of your income that is subject to income tax.
The exemption amounts are generally increased year by year, as adjusted for inflation, and the amount for tax year 2012 is $3,800. Each person for whom you claim an exemption must have a valid Social Security number or other valid tax identification number.

Since exemptions directly reduce your taxable income, ultimately, they will either increase your refund or reduce your tax liability. There are two types of exemptions: (a) *personal exemptions*, and (b) *exemptions for dependents*.

Your Personal Exemption

You can generally claim one exemption for yourself, and if you are married filing and a joint return, you may claim an exemption for your spouse. These are your personal exemptions. It is important to note that you can claim an exemption for your spouse only because you are married. Your spouse is never considered your dependent for tax purposes, and that is why an exemption for your spouse is considered a personal exemption.

It is very important to note that you <u>cannot</u> take a personal exemption for yourself if another person <u>can</u> claim you as a dependent. Note also, that even if that other person who could claim you did not do so, you still <u>cannot</u> claim your personal exemption.

If you are married, the rules for claiming the personal exemption for your spouse are as follows:

- You can claim one exemption for your spouse if you file a joint return with your spouse.
- If you are filing separately from your spouse, you can claim one exemption for your spouse, but ONLY if your spouse: (a) has no gross income, (b) filed no tax return, and (c) was not the dependent of another taxpayer. In tax law, your spouse in never considered your dependent.
- If you are divorced or legally separated at the end of the tax year, you cannot claim the exemption for your former spouse.
- If your spouse died during the year, and you would have been able to file a joint return with your spouse, you can still claim an exemption for your deceased spouse, provided you did not remarry before the end of the year.

Note that if you're filing MFS, and your spouse could be claimed as someone else's dependent, you cannot claim you spouse's exemption, even if the other taxpayer does not claim the exemption for your spouse.

If you are a non-resident alien, generally you can only claim an exemption for yourself. You cannot claim an exemption for your spouse or any dependents.

Exemptions for Your Dependents

You are allowed one exemption for each person you claim as a dependent on your tax return. Even if your dependent files a return, you still may be able to claim a personal exemption for him or her.

Your dependent must be either your *qualifying child* or your *qualifying relative*, and **must** have a valid identifying number. This number can be any of the following:

- Social Security number
- Individual taxpayer Identification number
- Adoption Taxpayer identification number

Three critical tests, however, must be met before you can claim them as a dependent.

The Dependent Taxpayer Test

If you could be claimed as a dependent by another taxpayer, you cannot claim anyone as a dependent on your tax return. This is true even if you have a qualifying child or qualifying relative. Also, if you file a joint return with your spouse, and can be claimed as a dependent by someone else, you and your spouse cannot claim anyone as a dependent on your joint return.

The Joint Return Test

Generally, you cannot claim a married person as a dependent if he or she files a joint return. However, if the married person filed the joint return only to claim a tax refund, and a tax liability would not exist for either spouse on separate returns, then you can claim that person as a dependent if all the other conditions are met.

The Citizen or Resident Test

You cannot claim a person as a dependent unless that person is a U.S. citizen, U.S. resident, U.S. national, or a resident of Canada or Mexico for some part of the year.

If you are a U.S. citizen or national who has legally adopted a child who is not a U.S. citizen, resident alien, or national, this test is met if the child lived as a member of your household the entire tax year.

Claiming a Qualifying Child

As already mentioned above, your dependent must be either your *qualifying child* or your *qualifying relative*. For your dependent to qualify as a *Qualifying Child*, five tests must be met. These tests are as follows:

The Relationship Test

For a child to be your Qualifying Child, that child must be related to you in one of the ways described below.

- The child must be your son, daughter, stepchild, eligible foster child, or a descendant of any of them. The child can also be your brother, sister, half-brother, half-sister, stepbrother, stepsister, or a descendant of any of them. (Therefore, this includes a niece or nephew, but not a cousin.)
- The child can be an adopted child. An adopted child is always treated as your own child, and therefore qualifies under the relationship test. The term, adopted child includes a child who was lawfully placed with you for adoption.
- An eligible foster child also qualifies under the relationship test, and is a child who has been placed with you by an authorized placement agency, or by judgment, decree, or other order of any court or competent jurisdiction.

The Age Test

To meet the age test the following must apply:

- The child must be under the age of 19 at the end of the tax year, and must be younger than you (or your spouse, if filing a joint return).
- If the child is older than 19, he or she must be a full-time student, but must be under the age of 24 at the end of the tax year, and younger than you (or your spouse, if filing a joint return). To qualify, the child must be a student during some part of any five calendar months of the year.
- If the child is permanently and totally disabled at any time during the year, the age test does not apply, and you will be able to claim the child as a dependent regardless of age.

The Residency Test

To satisfy the residency test, the general rule is that the child must have lived with you, sharing the same principal place of abode or home, for more than half of the year. There are, however, some exceptions to the general rule, and these apply in the following situations:

- In the case of temporary absences.
- For children who were born or died during the year.
- For kidnapped children.
- For children of divorced or separated parents.

(a) Temporary absences: If you, or your child, have to be temporarily absent from the home due to special circumstances such as illness, education, business, vacation, or military service, this is treated as a period of temporary absence. Under this exception, your dependent is considered to have lived with you during the periods of time when either you or your dependent had to be absent from the home, so you will be able to claim the child.

(b) Child born or died during year: If your child was born during the year, or died during the year, he or she is treated as having lived with you for the entire year, if your home was the child's home the entire time he or she was alive during the year. Consequently, you may be able to claim an exemption for a child who was born alive during the year, even if the child lived only for a moment. State or local law must treat the child as having been born alive. There must be proof of a live birth shown by an official document, such as a birth certificate. You must attach a copy of the child's birth certificate, death certificate, or hospital records to the return. The child must be your qualifying child or qualifying relative, and all the other tests to claim an exemption for a dependent must be met. You cannot claim an exemption for a stillborn child.

(c) Kidnapped child: If your child was kidnapped, you can treat the child as meeting the residency test, and claim the child. However, both of the following statements must be true: (a) the child is presumed by law enforcement authorities to have been kidnapped by someone who is <u>not</u> a member of your family or the child's family, and (b) in the year the kidnapping occurred, the child lived with you for more than half of the part of the year before the date of the kidnapping. This treatment applies for all years until the child is returned. However, the last year this treatment can apply is the earlier of: (a) the year there is a determination that the child is dead, or (b) the year the child would have reached age 18.

(d) Children of divorced or separated parents: If you are separated from your spouse, and the child lives with your spouse, that makes you the non-custodial parent. Tax law, however, states that the child can be treated as your qualifying child, if <u>all</u> the following apply:

- You and your spouse are divorced or legally separated under a decree of divorce or legal separation; are separated under a written separation agreement, or you lived apart from your spouse at all times during the last 6 months of the year.
- Your child received over half of his or her support for the year from you and your spouse.
- Your child was in the custody of you or your spouse for more than half of the year.
- The decree of divorce, or separate maintenance, or written separation agreement provides that you, the non-custodial parent can claim the child as a dependent, or your spouse signs a written declaration, such as Form 8332, *Release/Revocation of Release of Claim to Exemption for Child by Custodial Parent*, stating that he or she will not claim the child as a dependent for that year.

The Support Test
This is a simple test, which states that the child cannot have provided for more than half of his or her support for the year, if he or she is to be your qualifying child. For example, you provided $5,000 toward your 16-year-old son's support for the year. He has a part-time job and provided $7,000 to his own support. Since he provided more than half of his own support for the year, he is not your qualifying child, and you cannot claim him.
Note however, that a child who provides over half of his or her own support may still be a qualifying child when it comes to the earned income credit (EIC).

<u>The Special Test for Qualifying Child of More than One Person (Tiebreaker Rules)</u>

If your child meets the relationship, age, residence, and support test for you and another person(s), tax law allows only <u>one</u> person to claim the child as a qualifying child.

You and the other person(s) will therefore have to agree on who will claim the child for a particular year. If you and the other person(s) cannot agree on who will claim the child, the IRS *tiebreaker* rules will then come into effect, and will decide who will claim the child. The tiebreaker rules state that:

- If only one of the persons is the child's parent, the child is the qualifying child of the parent.
- If two of the persons are parents of the child and they do not file a joint return together, the child is the qualifying child of the parent with whom the child lived for the <u>longer</u> period of time during the year.
- If the two persons are parents of the child and they do not file a joint return together, and the child lived with each parent the same amount of time during the year, the child is the qualifying child of the parent with the highest adjusted gross income.
- If none of the persons are the child's parents, only the person with the highest AGI can treat the child as a qualifying child.

Claiming a Qualifying Relative

There are five tests to determine if you can claim a person as your Qualifying Relative. These tests are as follows:

<u>The Not a Qualifying Child Test</u>

If a child meets all the tests to be <u>your</u> qualifying child, that child <u>cannot</u> also be your Qualifying Relative. Also, if that child qualifies to be the Qualifying Child of another person, you cannot claim that child as your Qualifying Relative. For instance, you can't take the qualifying relative exemption for your child if:

- The child is a full-time college student, lives with you, and meets all the tests to be your qualifying child.
- The child lives with your parents and meets all the tests to be **their** qualifying child.

<u>The Member of Household or Relationship Test</u>

For you to claim a person as your Qualifying Relative, that person must either be:
- Related to you, or

31

- Be a member of your household for the entire year.

(a) Persons related to you: Persons related to you under tax law, include the following: your child, step-child, eligible foster child, brother, sister, half-brother, half-sister, stepbrother, stepsister, father, mother, grandparent, stepfather, stepmother, son-in-law, daughter-in-law, father-in-law, mother-in-law, brother-in-law, sister-in-law, or a descendant of any of these. Qualifying relatives who are related in one of these ways do <u>not</u> need to live with the taxpayer. As long as you meet the other four tests (gross income, support, citizenship, joint return), you can claim any of these qualifying relatives as a dependent. Also, relationships established by marriage do not end with death or divorce. So, if you support your mother-in-law, you can still claim her as a dependent even if you and your spouse are divorced.

(b) Member of your household: You can claim as a dependent on your tax return, any person who is a member of your household, even if you are not related to that person (as defined above). To qualify as a member of household, however, the person must meet the following tests:

- The person is a member of your household, and
- The person lives with you for an <u>entire</u> year, and
- The relationship between you and the dependent does not violate local law.

This means, then, that you may be able to claim a cousin, friend, boyfriend or girlfriend, or domestic partner, as a dependent under the qualifying relative tests. These qualifying relatives must, however, live with you for an entire year, and must meet all the other criteria for qualifying relatives (gross income, support, citizenship, joint return).

Note that your child who does not qualify to be a Qualifying Child because of not meeting the age test (over 19, and not in college, or over age 24) can be your Qualifying Relative, if all the other tests are met.

The Gross Income Test

You cannot claim a person as a Qualifying Relative if he or she had gross income for the tax year of $3,900 or more (the amount of one dependency exemption). This is true even if you provided most or all of that person's support. Gross income is defined as all income in the form of money, property, and services that is not exempt from tax. Gross income includes unemployment compensation and certain scholarships, but does not include welfare benefits and nontaxable Social Security.

If your relative's income includes income from rental property, you must treat total receipts as gross income; do not deduct taxes, repairs, etc.

The Support Test
Since a dependent is perceived to be someone you support, that person should not be making enough money to support himself or herself. You meet the support test if you can prove that you provide more than half of a person's total support for the entire year. Support includes amounts you spent to provide food, lodging, clothing, education, medical and dental care, recreation, transportation, and similar necessities for your dependent.

You should not include the following in support:

- Federal, state, and local income taxes paid by persons from their own income.
- Social Security and Medicare taxes paid by persons from their own income.
- Life insurance premiums.
- Funeral expenses.
- Scholarships received by a full-time student.
- Survivors' and dependents' educational assistance payments used for the support of the child who received them.

Any state amounts received, such as welfare, food stamps, and housing, are considered provided by the state for the person's support, and not by you.

If you are involved in a multiple support arrangement, where no one individually provides more than half of the dependent's support, but all collectively do, you have to agree among yourselves who will claim the exemption. The person claiming the exemption, however, must have provided more than 10% of the dependent's support.

In figuring support, you must compare the amount you contributed to the person's support with the total amount of support the person received from all other sources. This includes the person's own funds used for support. A person's own funds are not counted towards his support unless they are actually spent for support. Also, in figuring a person's total support, you should include tax-exempt income, savings, and borrowed amounts used to support that person.

The Citizenship Test
To claim a person as Qualifying Relative, that person must be a citizen or resident alien of the United States, Canada, or Mexico.

Other Points to Consider
It is very important to note that a person who is your Qualifying Relative only because he or she lives with you all year as a member of your household (not related to you), **cannot** qualify you to claim the HOH filing status. For

example, your girlfriend or boyfriend, who lives with you, or their children, cannot qualify you for the HOH filing status. You may however, claim the dependent exemption if they lived with you for the entire year, and all the other tests are met.

The Earned Income Credit

The *earned income credit* (EIC) is a tax credit that is specifically designed for lower income working families and individuals. The amount of the credit varies depending on your level of income and how many dependents you support. You can claim this credit with or without qualifying children, but greater tax credit is given to those who have qualifying children. This credit can be valued at close to $6,000 if you have three or more qualifying children. The earned income credit is a refundable credit, which means that you will receive a tax refund whether or not you had any taxable income.

As the name implies, the earned income credit is provided as an incentive for individuals to work. Consequently, to qualify for this credit, you must have some form of earned income during the year. Earned income includes wages you get from working, and income you earn from self-employment.

Defining Earned Income

The types of earned income that will qualify you for the earned income credit includes the following:

- Wages, salaries, and tips.
- Net earnings from self-employment.
- Gross income received as a statutory employee.
- Nontaxable combat pay (if the taxpayer elects to include it in earned income). You are given the choice to elect to have your nontaxable combat pay included in earned income for purposes of claiming the earned income credit. Your nontaxable combat pay is reported in box 12 of your Form W-2, with the code "Q".
- Long-term disability benefits. Disability benefits received from an employer's disability retirement plan are considered earned income until you reach minimum retirement age.

The following income is not considered earned income when figuring the earned income credit:

- Interest and dividends.
- Pension and annuities.

- Social Security and retirement benefits.
- Alimony and child support.
- Welfare benefits.
- Worker's compensation and unemployment compensation.
- Employee compensation that is nontaxable while taxpayer is an inmate.

Who Can Claim the Earned Income Credit?

To be eligible to claim the earned income credit, both your **earned income** and your **adjusted gross income** must be within certain ranges (see below). The amount of the credit varies, based on your earned income and on how many qualifying children you are supporting in your household. Note also, that you may qualify for this credit even if you do not have a qualifying child.

The following rules apply when claiming the earned income credit:

- You, your spouse (if married filing jointly), and your qualifying children must have valid Social Security numbers.
- You <u>must</u> have some form of earned income, either from employment or from self-employment. If you are married, at least one spouse must work and have earned income.
- You must be a U.S. citizen or resident alien all year. A nonresident alien married to a U.S. citizen or resident alien, and filing a joint return, may also claim the credit.
- You <u>cannot</u> claim the credit if you are married, and your filing status is MFS.
- You **cannot** claim the credit if you are a qualifying child of another person.
- You cannot claim the credit if you file Form 2555 or 2555-EZ (relating to foreign earned income).
- You cannot claim the credit if your investment income for 2012 exceeds $3,200. (Investment income includes taxable and nontaxable interest income, dividend income, and net capital gains income).

Claiming the EIC With Qualifying Children

You will not be eligible to claim the credit if your qualifying child is also the qualifying child of another person with a higher AGI.

For your qualifying child to make you eligible to claim the credit, he or she must meet <u>all</u> of the following four tests:

(a) Relationship test: The child must be related to you by birth, marriage, adoption, or foster arrangement. Consequently, the child can be your son, daughter, stepchild, eligible foster child, brother, sister, stepbrother, stepsister, or a descendant of any of the above. An eligible foster child must be a child placed with you by an authorized agency.

(b) Age test: The child must be: (a) under 19 at the end of the year, (b) under 24 at the end of the year, <u>and</u> a full time student, or (c) permanently and totally disabled at any time during the tax year regardless of age.

(c) Joint return test: The child must not have filed a joint return with their spouse, unless filing <u>only</u> for a tax refund, and would have no tax liability if separate returns were filed.

(d) Residency test: The qualifying child must live with you in the United States for more than half of the year (12 months for a foster child).

Note that a qualifying child cannot be used by more than one person to claim the EIC. If two or more persons can claim the same qualifying child, both persons must choose between themselves who will claim the credit. If they cannot agree who will claim the child as a qualifying child, the IRS will apply the tiebreaker rules.

Claiming the EIC Without Qualifying Children

You can claim the earned income credit even if you do not have a qualifying child, but the following rules apply:

- You must be over 25 years old, but less than 65 years old at the end of the tax year. (If filing MFJ, only one spouse needs to meet the age test.)
- You (and your spouse, if filing a joint return) cannot be a dependent on another person's tax return.
- You cannot be a qualifying child of another person.
- You must have lived in the United States for more than half of the year.

How to Figure the Credit

The amount of earned income credit you can claim depends on a number of factors, which include your income, your filing status, and whether you have: (a) no qualifying children, (b) one qualifying child, (c) two qualifying children, or (d) three or more qualifying children.

For tax year 2013, to qualify for the EIC, both your **earned income** and **modified adjusted gross income** must be less than:

- $14,340 ($19,680 if married filing jointly) if you have no qualifying children.
- $37,870 ($43,210 if married filing jointly) if you have one qualifying child.
- $43,038 (48,378 if married filing jointly) if you have two qualifying children.
- $46,227 ($51,567 if married filing jointly) if you have three or more qualifying children.

For Tax year 2013 the maximum credit is:

- $487 with no qualifying children.
- $3,250 with one qualifying child.
- $5,372 with two qualifying children.
- $6,044 with three or more qualifying children.

How to Claim the Credit

Because of the potential magnitude of this credit, the IRS pays a lot of attention to taxpayers who claim the earned income credit. This is because of the high incidence of fraudulent returns taxpayers have prepared to benefit from this credit. Consequently, if you wish to claim this credit, you must comply with the following requirements:

- Answer the earned income credit eligibility questions.
- Complete the Earned Income Credit Worksheet.
- If you have qualifying children, you must complete Schedule EIC, *Earned Income Credit*, and attach it to your tax return.

(Off the shelf tax software, such as Turbo Tax, will facilitate the completion of the above worksheets and schedules, and will figure the amount of the credit for inclusion on your tax return.)

To claim the earned income credit, you **must** file a tax return; you must do so even if you did not earn enough money that would require you to file a return. You can use Form 1040EZ to claim the credit if you do not have a qualifying child. You claim your EIC on line 64a of Form 1040.

Because of the nature and potential value of this credit, the IRS may ask you to provide documents to prove that you are entitled to the earned income credit.

These may include birth certificates, school records, medical records, etc., so it would be wise to have these handy.

The Child Tax Credit

The child tax credit is a credit given for each dependent child on your tax return, who is under the age of 17 at the end of the tax year. The child tax credit is a nonrefundable credit, and is intended to provide an extra measure of tax relief for taxpayers with qualifying children.

How to Qualify for the Child Tax Credit

To qualify for this credit, you must have a qualifying child on your tax return. The rules for determining if your child is a qualifying child for the purpose of this credit are as follows:

- The child must be your son, daughter, adopted child, stepchild, eligible foster child, brother, sister, stepbrother, stepsister, or a descendant of any of them. (This includes your niece, nephew, grandchild, great-grandchild, etc.)
- The child must not provide for over half of his or her own support for the year.
- The child must be a citizen or resident of the United States.
- The child must be under the age of 17 on the last day of the tax year.
- Generally, you must claim the child as a dependent on your tax return.
- The child must have lived with you for more than half of the year.
- The child must be younger than you.
- The child must not have filed a joint return, unless the joint return was filed only to claim a tax refund, and no tax liability would have existed on separate returns.

An adopted child qualifies be your qualifying child, even if the adoption is not final, as long as the child has been placed with you by an authorized agency for legal adoption.

An eligible foster child qualifies to be your qualifying child, as long as he or she was placed with you by an authorized placement agency, by judgment decree, or any other court of competent jurisdiction.

How to Claim the Child Tax Credit

The child tax credit allows you to claim up to $1,000 per qualifying child, and is claimed on line 51, Form 1040. If you cannot claim the entire amount of the credit on line 51, because your tax is lower than the credit, and cannot absorb the full amount of the credit, you may be able to claim the balance as a refundable *Additional Child Tax Credit* on line 65 (see below).

The Phase Out Amounts

The child tax credit is one of those credits, which begin to phase out after your income exceeds a certain amount. This credit begins to phase out when your modified adjusted gross income exceeds the following amounts for each filing status:

- MFJ - $110,000
- HOH, QW, or Single - $75,000
- MFS - $55,000

The credit will begin being reduced by $50 for every $1,000 that your income exceeds the above threshold amounts, so the *Child Tax Credit Worksheet* from IRS Publication 972 should be used to compute the actual amount of your child tax credit.

(Off the shelf tax software, such as TurboTax, will effectively complete this worksheet and include it in your tax return.)

The Additional Child Tax Credit

If you cannot claim the entire amount of your child tax credit because it exceeds your tax, you may be able to claim the unused portion as an **additional child tax credit**. The additional child tax credit is a refundable credit, and is available to you whenever you cannot claim the entire amount of the child tax credit on line 51 of Form 1040. You may be able to claim the unused amount on line 65 of Form 1040.
The amount of the refund, however, may differ depending on your total earned income. It may also be affected by the amount of Social Security and Medicare taxes that were paid.

Figuring and Claiming the Credit

The amount of the additional child tax credit that you can claim is the lower of:
- Your disallowed child tax credit.
- 15% of your earned income that exceeds $3,000.

You figure and claim this credit by completing Form 8812, *Additional Child Tax Credit*, and attaching it to Form 1040.

(Off the shelf tax software, such as Turbo Tax, will effectively complete this form and include it in your tax return).

The Credit for Child and Dependent Care Expenses

You may be able to claim a credit for *child and dependent care,* if you pay someone to care for your dependent child who is under the age of 13, or for your spouse or other dependent who is not able to care for himself or herself. You must have incurred this expenditure so that you (and your spouse, if you are married) could work or look for work. If you are married, both you and your spouse must have some form of earned income, unless one spouse either was a full-time student for 5 months of the tax year, or was physically or mentally incapable of self-care.

The child and dependent care credit, which is a nonrefundable credit, is claimed on line 48 of Form 1040, and is generally a percentage of the amount of the work-related child and dependent care expenses you paid to a care provider. The amount of this percentage depends on your adjusted gross income.

Defining Work-Related Expenses

The tax credit for child and dependent care expenses is intended only to assist those who incur these expenses in order to enable them to earn income. Therefore, you can only claim dependent care expenses that the IRS considers to be *work-related*. Dependent care expenses incurred are considered work-related <u>only</u> if they are: (a) incurred to allow the taxpayer to work or look for work, and (b) are for a qualifying person's care.

Qualifying work-related expenses include the following:

- *Household services*, if they are at least partly responsible for the well-being and protection of a qualifying person. These can include cleaning service, maid, cook, and housekeeper's wages, room and board.
- *Day care centers*, if the center complies with all state and local regulations.
- *Schooling*, if the child is in a grade below the first grade and the amount paid cannot be separated from the cost of care.

Defining Qualifying Persons

For you to claim child and dependent care expenses, your qualifying person must be one of three types:

- A child under age 13 when the care was provided, and whom you can claim as a dependent on your tax return.
- Your spouse who was physically or mentally incapable of self-care.
- Your dependent who was physically or mentally incapable of self-care, and for whom you can claim a dependent exemption, or could claim an exemption except that the person failed the gross income test (having a gross income of over $3,900).

To claim this credit, the qualifying person must have lived with you for more than half of the year. (There are exceptions for the birth or death of a qualifying person, or for a child of divorced or separated parents.)

The Requirements for Claiming the Credit

To be eligible to claim the credit, the expenses incurred must be for the qualifying person's well-being and protection; for example, placing your child in a day care center while you work or look for work.

To claim the credit, the following conditions must apply:

- The expenses incurred must be for the care of one or more qualified persons.
- You (and your spouse, if filing a joint return) must have some form of earned income from work performed during the year. Earned income includes employee compensation and net earnings from self-employment.
- If only one spouse has earned income, the IRS allows the other spouse to be treated as having earned income for any month he or she is: (a) a full time student (that is, a student for some part of each of 5 calendar months during the year), or (b) physically or mentally incapable of self-care (see below).
- The care must have been provided for the qualifying person so that you (and your spouse) can work or look for work.
- You must be paid for the work (must have earned income).
- Work also includes the process of actively looking for work, as long as you have some form of earned income during the year.
- The expenses for the care cannot be paid to any of the following persons: (a) your spouse, (b) the parent of your qualifying person, (c) someone you can claim as your dependent on your tax return, or (d)

your child who will not be age 19 or older by the end of the year, even if he or she is not your dependent.

- Your filing status must be Single, MFJ, HOH, or QW. You cannot claim this credit if you are filing MFS.
- You must identify the care provider on your tax return (see below).

A spouse who is either a full-time student, or who is not capable of self-care, is treated by the IRS as having earned income of $250 per month if there is one qualifying person, or $500 per month if there are two or more qualifying persons. This provision qualifies you to claim the credit even though your spouse has no earned income.

Figuring the Amount of the Credit

The amount of the work-related expenses that is eligible for the credit is limited to the lowest of these three amounts:

- The actual expenses you incurred.
- A dollar limit of $3,000 for one qualifying person; or $6,000 for two or more qualifying persons.
- Your earned income. (If you are filing a joint return, the earned income that you will use to do this comparison cannot be more than the smaller of each spouses' earned income.)

The qualifying expenses that you use to figure the credit must be reduced by the amount of any dependent care benefits provided by your employer that you exclude from your income. These amounts are shown in box 10 of your Form W-2.

The actual amount of the credit you receive is a percentage of the eligible work-related expenses you incurred. This ranges between 20% and 35% of your qualifying expenses, depending on your adjusted gross income, with the percentage decreasing as your income increases. For adjusted gross income above $43,000, the maximum credit you can claim is 20% of eligible expenses. Therefore, if you earn over $43,000, the maximum you can receive for this credit is $1,200 (20% of $6,000).

How to Claim the Credit

To claim the credit for child and dependent care expenses, you need to fill out Parts I and II of Form 2441, *Child and Dependent Care Expenses*. This form requires you to provide identification information (SSN or EIN) for the care provider(s) and the Social Security numbers of the qualifying children or disabled persons. The form helps you to compute your credit by comparing your allowable expenses with your wages and other earnings (and those of your spouse, if filing jointly). The amount of the credit, as figured on line 11 of Form 2441, is claimed on line 48 of Form 1040.

If your employer provided you with dependent care benefits, you must report this amount (which is shown in box 10 of your W-2) by completing Part III of Form 2441.

(Off the shelf tax software, such as Turbo Tax, will bring up Form 2441 for you to populate with the appropriate information, and the software will compute the amount to be included in your tax return.)

Note however, that if the information on Form 2441 is incomplete or incorrect, the IRS can disallow the credit, unless you can show due diligence in trying to provide the information.

Other Points to Consider

- You cannot claim work-related expenses paid for child and dependent care while you are off work due to illness. This applies even if you receive sick pay and is still considered an employee.

- You cannot claim transportation costs of getting a qualified person from home to the care location and back; this is not considered work-related expenses.

- If you pay someone to come to your home and care for your dependent or spouse, you may be considered a household employer, and may have to withhold and pay Social Security and Medicare tax, and also federal unemployment tax.

The Standard Deduction vs. Itemized Deduction

In preparing your tax returns, you are allowed the choice of either claiming the *standard deduction*, or claiming *itemized deductions*. Your deductions (standard or itemized) are subtracted from your adjusted gross income (AGI) to figure your taxable income. Depending on which choice gives you the greater benefit, you may choose to take your standard deduction, or you may choose to claim itemized deductions; the aim here is to maximize your refund or minimize your tax liability. The objective, then, is to provide you with relevant knowledge to enable you to make an informed decision whether you should take the standard deduction or whether you should claim itemized deductions.

What is the Standard Deduction

The standard deduction is a fixed dollar amount that the government allows taxpayers who do not itemize deductions to deduct from their income. The standard deduction reduces the amount of income that is taxed, and eliminates the need for many taxpayers to itemize deductions, because you can take the higher deduction of the two. This deduction is based on your filing status, and is available to U.S. citizens and resident aliens. It is not available to nonresident aliens residing in the United States.
The Standard Deduction may also include additional amounts for age and blindness.

The amount of your standard deduction generally depends on the following:

- Your filing status.
- Whether you are 65 or older and/or blind. (Your standard deduction is higher if you are over 65 years old, and/or blind.)
- Whether you can be claimed as a dependent on another person's tax return.

For tax year 2013, the standard deduction amounts for the various filing statuses are as follows:

- Single -$6,100
- MFJ - $12,200
- MFS - $6,100
- HOH - $8,950
- QW - $12,200

If you are 65 or older:

- Add another $1,200 to your standard deduction if your filing status is MFJ, QW or MFS.
- Add another $1,500 to your standard deduction if your filing status is Single or HOH.

If you are blind:

- Add another $1,200 to your standard deduction if your filing status is MFJ, QW or MFS.
- Add another $1,500 to your standard deduction if your filing status is Single or HOH.

You are not eligible to claim the standard deduction if any of the following situations apply to you.

- You and your spouse use the *Married Filing Separately* filing status, and your spouse itemizes deductions. In this case, you cannot claim the standard deduction, but must also itemize deductions.
- You are filing for a short year, due to a change in your annual accounting period.
- You were a nonresident or a dual-status alien during the year.

If you can be claimed as a dependent on another person's tax return, your standard deduction is limited to the greater of: (a) $950, or (b) your total earned income for the year plus $300 (but not exceeding $5,950).

What Are Itemized Deductions

You should itemize deductions if your total eligible expenses are more than the standard deduction amount. Also, you must itemize if you do not qualify for the standard deduction. Itemized deductions are comprised of certain eligible expenses that individual taxpayers in the United States can report on their federal income tax returns in order to decrease their taxable income. Most taxpayers are allowed a choice between the itemized deductions and the standard deduction.

To claim your itemized deductions, you must complete Schedule A, *Itemized Deductions*. You enter all your eligible expenses in the appropriate sections on Schedule A. The total of all your deductions on line 29 of Schedule A is then transferred to line 40 of Form 1040, to take the deduction.

The eligible expenses that you are allowed to claim on Schedule A, fall into the following broad categories:

- Medical and dental expenses.
- Taxes you paid.
- Interest you paid.
- Gifts to charity.
- Casualty and theft losses.
- Job expenses and certain miscellaneous deductions.
- Other miscellaneous deductions.

www.ingramcontent.com/pod-product-compliance
Lightning Source LLC
Chambersburg PA
CBHW081236170526
45165CB00009B/3075